The *Mema*
Sadie Mae Ferguson Hill
11/26/30 - 7/09/19

Copyright © 2020 Angie Hill Klein

angiekleinart.com

All rights reserved.

Library of Congress Control Number: 2020920028

Author - Angie Hill Klein
Illustrators - Shirley Hill Layton and Angie Hill Klein
Book Designer - Ellen Lynch Designs

ISBN: 9798695420524

Printed in the USA

A Time for Everything

¹ There is a time for everything, and a season for every activity under the heavens:

2   a time to be born and a time to die, a time to plant and a time to uproot,

4   a time to weep and a time to laugh, a time to mourn and a time to dance,

5   a time to scatter stones and a time to gather them, a time to embrace and a time to refrain from embracing

6   a time to search and a time to give up, a time to keep and a time to throw away,

7   a time to tear and a time to mend, a time to be silent and a time to speak,

8   a time to love and a time to hate, a time for war and a time for peace.

9 What do workers gain from their toil?

10 I have seen the burden God has laid on the human race.

11 He has made everything beautiful in its time. He has also set eternity in the human heart; yet no one can fathom what God has done from beginning to end.

Ecclesiastes 3:1-2, 4-11

Sadie Tells the Bees
by: Angie Hill Klein

Illustrations by: Shirley Hill Layton
& Angie Hill Klein

The History of Telling the Bees

"Telling the Bees" is an old tradition in which the bees were informed of any important events in the beekeeper's lives. It was believed that sharing the family news with the bees and treating them as part of the family in that way, kept the bees happy. If the custom was forgotten, the bees could leave their hives, stop producing honey or die. In many instances, the bees were spotted at their keeper's funerals and other family events, dutifully paying their respects. Although this harmonious, magical custom of "Telling the Bees" is most well known in England, it has also been recorded in Ireland, Germany, Whales, Netherlands, Switzerland, Bohemia and the United States.

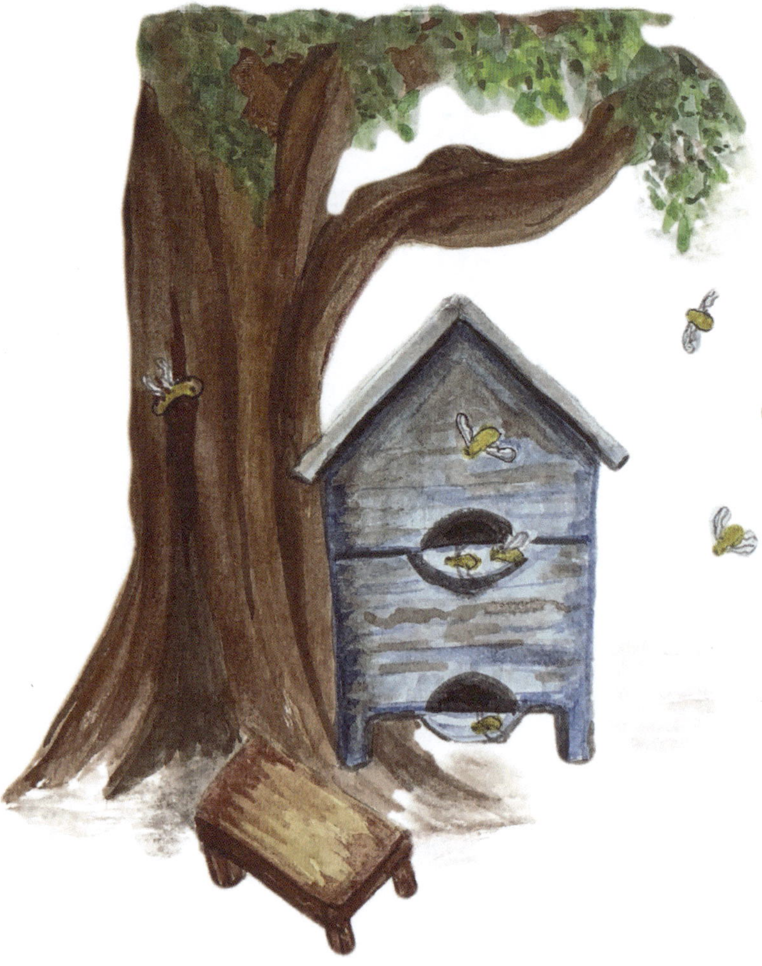

Sadie Tells the Bees

by Angie Hill Klein

In a very special spot, in the back corner of a quaint country yard, sat a hive of very busy bees. Up the hill, just beyond their hive, lay Sadie's family's farm. Sadie and her Grandaddy, Mema, Mama, and Daddy all shared a small wooden home there that had been in their family for many generations. For as long as Sadie's family worked their small plot of land, the bees worked just as hard right alongside them, intimately sharing the ins and outs of daily life on the farm.

In the field at the edge of the farm, rows upon rows of summer vegetables grew to feed the family, some even taller than Sadie. Green bean plants shot up from the ground. Their delicate white blossoms danced in the breeze, waiting for the bees to come pollinate them. Heavy melon flowers swayed in time, sending their pollen's sweet perfume into the wind. The plants called the bees and the bees always answered.

Sadie's family valued and respected the hard-working bees. Every evening at the dinner blessing, Sadie waited for her favorite part when Grandaddy added, "And thank you, Lord, for the bees and their part in your grand design. Without them, this meal would not be possible."

Sadie often snuck a peek at the window during that part of the prayer and always found a few bees by the window who seemed to be praying right along with them.

Sadie spent her summer days playing and ducking in and out of the flower gardens, often spotting Mama or Daddy, Mema or Grandaddy sitting on the small stool in front of the hives "telling the bees." One day, Sadie's Mama explained that for as long as the family could remember they had each sat on that same stool and told the bees of all the family news. Sadie's Mama told Sadie how the bees were the first to know when Uncle Jimmy was lost in the war and how the bees mourned right along with them. They were told of Mema's tired heart and they had been among the first to hear when Sadie's Mama and Daddy found out that she was on the way.

5

Sadie loved picturing her Mama and Daddy walking hand in hand, by the daisies, past the duck pond to the quiet corner where the bees lived. She imagined her Mama's soft voice sweetly telling the bees of their exciting news, "A baby is on the way!" Sadie could picture the bees dancing with joy on the edge of the hive, their wings fanning in unison, while Mama hugged her growing belly.

Sadie was fascinated by this part of their family history so she asked, "When will I tell the bees, Mama?" "You'll know when it's time Sadie," Mama replied. "And when you do, be sure to listen to them too." She kissed Sadie on the forehead and went back to doing her chores.

Sadie thought this was curious, but she went

on about her playing, wondering what her Mama meant by "listening to the bees."

Summer and fall came and went as usual. Sadie's family worked the land with the bees. Chores were done, meals were made, prayers were prayed. But as the chill of winter approached, Sadie noticed that Mema was slowing down. She sat in the kitchen in the early evenings, but she couldn't help Mama with the cooking anymore. Grandaddy had to hold Mema's hand to help her walk from place to place, and she spent more and more time in bed that winter.

Early one morning, just as spring arrived on the farm, Sadie was awakened by a small swarm of bees at her window. As she made her way down the hall, she noticed that something wasn't right. Her home seemed more still than normal. Breakfast wasn't cooking, and she couldn't hear her family loudly discussing the work that needed to be done that day. She stopped at the kitchen doorway and found only her Mama, Daddy, and Grandaddy sitting around the kitchen table. "Where is Mema?" Sadie wondered. Before she had a chance to ask, Sadie heard her Mama begin to pray in a broken voice, "We thank you Lord for taking Mama to heaven, but we will miss her."

Sadie didn't know quite what her Mama meant, but she knew it was very sad news.

Suddenly, Sadie remembered the stories her Mama told her and knew what she had to do. As she turned to leave, she caught her Mama's gaze for just a moment and heard her whisper "It's time," softly smiling through her tears.

Sadie ran as fast as she could, her bare feet jumping over fresh puddles and pushing through clumps of new spring flowers still wet with morning dew. She ran past the duck pond and came to a quick halt in front of the only place she could think to go. Once she reached the hives, she became a little nervous. Slowly she sat down on the little red stool and realized she was crying. Where should she begin?

One by one, the small golden bees started to emerge, resting on the edge of the hive. A soft hum grew. Sadie stammered, "Um, excuse me, please. There is something I need to tell. Mama said Mema went to heaven, but I'm not sure where that is."

The hum of the bees softened and one by one they put their heads down in a very deep bow. Sadie knew they understood and were sad too. She put her head down and let her own tears fall.

II

Sadie's cry was soon interrupted by a melodic little voice, soft but powerful. It almost seemed to come from inside her head. "Sadie, dear, we've been expecting you, but I'm sorry this was your first news to tell."

Sadie, startled, stood up from her stool and stepped forward for a closer look. There, in front of the bees, was the queen bee, larger and even lovelier than the worker bees. "You know me?" Sadie asked. "You can talk to me?"

"Yes, dear one," the queen replied. "We've always been able to talk to your family and we began with each one when they were about your age. We knew you would be coming soon."

Sadie, so amazed by the queen, almost forgot why she was there. The tear running down her cheek reminded her. She asked the queen, "Why did Mema have to leave?"

The queen thought for a moment. "God calls each one of us in His own time to be with Him in heaven," she softly replied. "God called your Mema to Heaven. This was the time He picked for her before she was even born. But Sadie, I want to share a secret with you. Your Mema is much closer than you think. Heaven is all around us."

Sadie looked around, squinting and blinking, seeing only the big, old oak tree and the hives it shaded. Sadie thought the queen might be wrong. When grown-ups talked about heaven, it always seemed to be a place far, far away, beyond the clouds.

The queen could see that Sadie was doubting her. "You're looking with your eyes Sadie," she said. "Ask God to help you look with your heart."

"When you miss your Mema, little one, feel her warm hug as you lie in the meadow letting the sun warm your cheeks. Hear her laughter when you see a new spring calf learning to walk. See her smile in the sunflowers as they follow the sun. When you need to hear her say 'I love you', look for the butterflies. They carry the 'I love you's' from heaven."

"I will try to look with my heart," Sadie promised, "but what do I do now?"

"It's time for you to go back to the house and be with your family, but you'll come to visit us often, Sadie. You'll tell us the family news and about school when you start this year. We'll tell you when it's time to harvest the extra honey and we'll let you know when the weather is changing or when the land needs a little extra care, just like we did for your Mema and your Mama before you."

Sadie said goodbye to her new friends the bees and slowly made her way up to the porch, where her Mama was sitting in the swing, waiting to give her an extra-long hug.

"Did you tell the bees?" Mama asked.

"I did," replied Sadie "and I listened too."

That spring was a little different for Sadie's family. It was a little sad at times, but the daily work of life on the farm continued as usual and kept Sadie busy.

One afternoon when Sadie was especially missing her Mema, she started pondering all that the queen bee had said and decided to give it a try. She headed outside to look for heaven, hoping to see her Mema there. As she started out the door, she prayed, "Lord, help me to see heaven with my heart today."

Sadie had only taken a few steps into the flower garden before she saw a bright red ladybug sitting on a flower. She leaned in for a closer look, and before she knew it, the ladybug flew up and landed on her nose!

"Lord, help me to see heaven with my heart today."

19

Sadie couldn't help but giggle, which reminded her of her Mema's laugh and how it had always made her laugh too.

Next, Sadie went to the duck pond to look for Mema's hug. On the bank sat a Mama duck, who was cleaning her new baby's soft feathers. This reminded Sadie of Mema brushing her hair in the mornings and of all the talks they shared.

Elated, Sadie stood up, stretched her arms wide, and twirled. She shouted into the wind, "Thank you, Lord! I love you, Mema!" Sadie twirled and twirled until she fell into the grass. Then, out of nowhere, as if carried on the breeze, a delicate, bright blue butterfly fluttered up to Sadie and danced in front of her. Sadie smiled brightly.

She knew then that the bees were right. Heaven is all around us. You just have to listen to the bees and look with your heart.

Printed in Great Britain
by Amazon